Larry Brandy

contents

Welcome to Wiradjuri Country

My name is Larry Brandy and I'm a Wiradjuri man from Condobolin, in central New South Wales. Australia has more than 500 Aboriginal Nations. The Wiradjuri Nation is just one of them, but our Country covers a huge area in New South Wales. The only other Nation whose Country covers a larger area is the Pitjanjatjara Nation of Central Australia.

Today, most Wiradjuri people live in towns and cities, and we are reclaiming Wiradjuri traditions, stories and language.

murri-yang
sky world

Wambuul
Macquarie River

Milawa
Murray River

People of the three rivers

Wiradjuri Country stretches from the Great Dividing Range in the east, where the rainbow serpent sleeps, to the west, past the central New South Wales towns of Bathurst and Orange, to Hillston and Hay. Wiradjuri Country also goes north beyond the towns of Dubbo and Gilgandra and south to Albury.

The Wiradjuri are known as the people of the three rivers—**Wambuul** (the Macquarie River), **Galari** (the Lachlan River) and **Marrambidya** (the Murrumbidgee River). We also border **Milawa** (the Murray River).

Rivers are very important to us. So are woodlands, grasslands and all the other habitats that make up our Country. **Murri-yang** (the sky world) is also part of our Country. Star constellations tell us when to collect particular foods and how to find our way around Country.

Galari
Lachlan River

Marrambidya
Murrumbidgee River

Wiradjuri plants and animals

We taught our **buraay** (children) what was good to eat or hunt, what was good for medicine and what was poisonous. We taught our children to respect and listen to their Elders. Many plants in the bush are poisonous so children must not eat a plant unless an Elder says they can. We never killed anything for fun, but when we did kill an animal we didn't waste anything. We relied on plants and animals, so we respected them and learnt from them.

Our **buraay** learnt how to look after Country—which we call **nguram-bang**—so that the plants and animals never disappeared. Wiradjuri people knew a lot about where to find plants and animals, how animals behave and how to identify animal tracks. We also knew how to manage Country using fire and farming. We were farmers as well as hunters and scientists.

Wiradjuri names

Each Aboriginal Nation has their own language. In the Wiradjuri language, the name for the wedge-tailed eagle is **maliyan**, whereas around Melbourne in Wurundjuri Country it is called 'bunjil'.

Many of the names we have for birds sound like their call. For example, **ngugug**, our name for the boobook owl sounds like its call, so does our name for the willy wagtail, **dyirri-dyirri**. Even our name for the laughing kookaburra, which is **gugu-ba-rra**, sounds like its call if you repeat it slowly.

From the 1770s, when the early European explorers and scientists first arrived in Australia, there were plants and animals that they had never seen before. They gave them new common names. Many names, such as kangaroo, kookaburra and wombat, came from the Aboriginal language of the area, but others were based on animals that lived in Europe, such as robin and magpie.

gugu-ba-rra
laughing kookaburra

Wiradjuri stories

In recent times, we have lost some of our stories or parts of stories. Sometimes this was because older Wiradjuri people were not allowed to speak their language or were separated from their families. The stories were not written down, so they couldn't be shared with the next generation.

A constellation in the sky or features on the land, such as rocks and mountains, can remind us of a story. Our **buraay** learn about different plants and animals through stories. Aboriginal people were among the first astronomers in the world and had names and stories for the constellations in the sky.

There are many stories from **balanda** (the beginning), which tell us how the mountains and rocks were formed. The rainbow serpent and the bunyip are in many stories. **Waawii** is the bunyip of deep waterholes. The rainbow serpent formed the mountains and created the rivers.

We tell stories like 'Tiddalik the giant frog' to our children so that in the future they can tell them to their children. This means that we'll never lose our stories.

Take time to learn about your country and your plant and animal neighbours. You may even discover signs of Aboriginal people who lived in your area before you. Scarred trees, middens, rock art and axe-grinding grooves show you that Aboriginal people have lived there or passed through. The Australian landscape was changed by Aboriginal people as we burnt and farmed **nguram-bang**.

Come on a journey with me into Wiradjuri Country to learn about this part of Australia and the wonderful plants and animals that live here with us.

rivers

Wiradjuri are the people of the three **bila** (rivers). Their names are **Galari** (the Lachlan River), **Wambuul** (the Macquarie River) and **Marrambidya** (the Murrumbidgee River). **Milawa** (the Murray River) borders our Country. We have a deep connection with these rivers. Many of our stories are linked to rivers and the animals that live there.

Billabong comes from the Wiradjuri word **bila-bang**—**bila** for river and **bang** is from the word **banga**, which means 'breaking off'. So, a billabong is a part of a river that has broken off from the main part. The word **bila-bang** is also used for the Milky Way.

The rivers are the bloodlines of **nguram-bang** (Country). They are as important to **nguram-bang** as our blood is to us. Our **bali** (babies) used to be born close to rivers. The rivers provided clean water for drinking and washing in, and they gave us plants and animals for our food and medicines. The trees gave us shelter.

We made **muriin** (canoes) from the bark of large trees. If you look carefully along river banks, you can see trees that have a large scar, showing where a canoe has been cut out of the bark. To push the canoes along the rivers, we used long sticks.

We traded stones, for making **guwingal** (stone axes), and ochre, with other Wiradjuri clans and neighbouring Aboriginal Nations. We liked to have types of rock that we couldn't find in Wiradjuri Country and ochre in colours that we didn't have.

We also fished from canoes and ate our catch in spots along the river banks. Sometimes, today, you can see middens in these places. Middens are piles of old mussel shells and fish and turtle bones—the leftovers of meals eaten by generations of Wiradjuri people.

Today, our rivers are not healthy. Fish called carp were introduced to Australia by European settlers a long time ago and now they are a pest. They have turned many of the clear rivers to a milky brown. Dams have been built on the rivers, and farmers take river water to irrigate their crops. Dams and irrigation have changed the flow of the rivers and the amount of water in the rivers.

animals

Bila-durang
Platypus

bila-durang
platypus

muriin
bark canoe

bila
river

burrow

deadly facts

Bila-durang

... close their eyes, ears and nose when swimming under the water.

... can hold their breath under the water for up to two and a half minutes.

... live alone in burrows in river banks.

... use their sensitive bill to find tiny prey under the water.

... don't have teeth.

... lay one or two eggs. The babies are tiny and naked when they break through their shell.

... babies lap up milk that oozes through the mother's belly skin.

Wiradjuri people call the platypus **bila-durang**. **Bila**, our word for river, shows that the platypus is a river animal.

Stories about **bila-durang** tell us that the platypus is part duck (bird) and part water rat (mammal). She has webbed feet and a bill and lays eggs like a bird, but she has fur like a mammal.

One **bila-durang** story about a young duck taught children to listen to their Elders. The young duck's parents tell her not to swim down the river, but she does anyway. **Munun** the water rat kidnaps her. Luckily, she escapes and returns home. Later, she has babies that are different to the other ducks' babies, so she's not allowed to stay. She's very sad and takes her babies to the cooler rivers. Here they thrive because they have fur. Today, platypuses are found only in the east of Wiradjuri Country, in the cooler rivers.

We never hunted **bila-durang** or ate her eggs, probably because we knew that she wasn't as common as other animals. We believed that it was a good omen to see a platypus.

Wiradjuri people have always known a lot about **bila-durang**, but the Europeans, who first arrived in Australia over 200 years ago, had never seen anything like it. Captain John Hunter, the second Governor of New South Wales, sent a specimen and a drawing of the platypus back to England. Scientists there thought that the animal was a fake. They believed that someone had sewn the bill and feet of a duck onto a mammal to trick them.

munun
water rat

bila
river

yaanharra
spear with three prongs

muriin
bark canoe

Gagalin

Yellow Belly (Golden Perch)

Wiradjuri people love to fish. We made **yaanharra** (spears with three prongs), which helped to keep hold of the fish. We also fished from **muriin** (bark canoes). At night we lit a small fire in the canoe to attract fish to the surface of the water. We could then easily catch them.

We used **barrinan**, a plant we found in small **bila-bang** (billabongs), and crushed its leaves and put them in the water. The leaves took oxygen out of the water, stunning the fish. When they floated to the surface, we took only as many as we needed. After a while, the rest of the fish recovered and swam away.

gagalin
yellow belly

One of our favourite fish was **gagalin** (yellow belly) and it still is today. It's also called golden perch. The best time to look for **gagalin** is in spring when **bila** (the rivers) are flowing. **Gagalin** are getting harder to find because there are now so many introduced carp in the rivers.

Gagalin

... can grow to 40–50cm long and can weigh about 5kg.

... live in deep slow-flowing parts of rivers, billabongs and lakes.

... eat other fish species and yabbies.

... swim hundreds of kilometres up rivers to lay their eggs.

barrinan
small shrub

bila-bang
billabong

gudhamang-dhuray
having turtles

gudhamang
eastern long-necked turtle

Gudhamang
Eastern Long-necked Turtle

Gudhamang was an important source of food for us. We ate the turtle and also her eggs. Of course, we left some of the eggs to hatch. The shell became a container and we used it to boil food and medicine on the fire.

The eastern long-necked turtle is the most widespread turtle in Wiradjuri Country, but we also ate other turtles that lived in **nguram-bang** (Country)—**warramba** (Murray turtle) and **gandhalwurr** (broad-shelled turtle).

The town of Cootamundra gets its name from the word **gudhamang-dhuray**, which means 'having turtles'.

Gudhamang

- *... live in rivers, dams, lakes and wetlands.*
- *... make a nest for their eggs by digging a hole, close to the water.*
- *... have a long neck that looks a bit like a snake. They use their neck to strike out at their prey (such as tadpoles, small fish, frogs, worms and insects).*
- *... may walk across land to search for water or they may dig themselves into mud or under a log until the rain comes.*

Yabi

Common Yabby

Wiradjuri people love to catch and eat **yabi** (yabbies, freshwater crayfish), especially in the warmer months of spring and summer, when **yabi** are more active. **Buraay** (children) dangle small bits of meat in the water to attract the yabbies to the surface and then scoop them up with small nets. They cook the yabbies in the coals of a fire.

deadly facts Yabi

... live in still water, preferably muddy water, because it helps to protect them from predators such as fish and birds.

... may travel over land for long distances to find water or they may bury themselves and wait for rain.

... have two large pincers, which they use to carry water plants and small dead animals to their mouth.

... have a hard shell covering their body. To grow, they shed this shell. Underneath is a new larger shell.

... lay hundreds of eggs, which the females keep under their tail for a few weeks until the eggs hatch.

yabi
common yabby

deadly facts Budhanbang

- ... *live in wetlands and along most rivers in Australia.*
- ... *are dark brown, even though their English name is 'Pacific black duck'.*
- ... *eat mainly the seeds of water plants, but they also eat insects, shells and other small invertebrates. To feed, they have to turn themselves upside down in the water so that all you can see are their tails sticking up.*
- ... *breed only when there's enough food and water. They have lots of ducklings, but not many survive.*

Budhanbang

Pacific Black Duck

Wiradjuri people call the Pacific black duck **budhanbang**. To hunt these birds, we used **bargan**, the boomerang that flies back to the hunter. Some hunters stood on each side of a small **bila** (river). Further down the river, others stretched a net over the water between two trees.

The hunt began when a hunter threw his **bargan**. The **bargan** made a whistling sound in the air like a hawk, so the ducks became frightened and started to fly down the river. The other hunters along the river also threw their **bargan**. The ducks, thinking there was a hawk above them, stayed low over the water and flew straight into the net down the river.

dinawan
emu

gugaa
goanna

bila-bang
billabong

bila
river

bandhaa
red kangaroo

galin-dulin
eel

let me tell you a story

Tiddalik the giant frog

buraay
child

wilay
common brushtail possum

balanda
beginning

gugu-ba-rra
laughing kookaburra

wambad
wombat

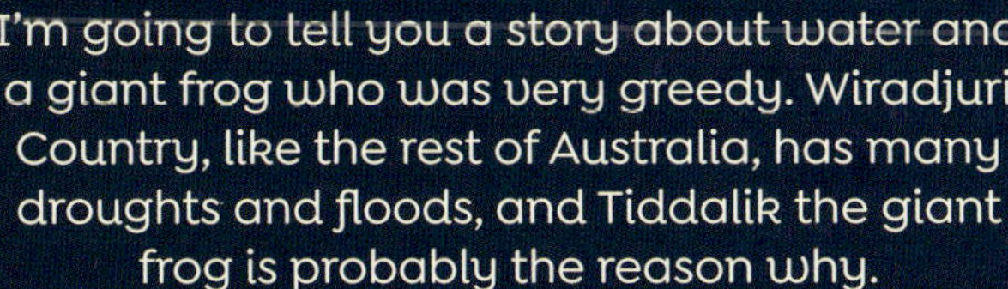

I'm going to tell you a story about water and a giant frog who was very greedy. Wiradjuri Country, like the rest of Australia, has many droughts and floods, and Tiddalik the giant frog is probably the reason why.

Long ago in **balanda**—the beginning—long before people roamed Earth, there lived an enormous frog called Tiddalik. He was the biggest frog to ever have lived. Bigger than **bandhaa** the red kangaroo, bigger than a dinosaur, bigger than Uluru, the big red rock.

One morning, in the middle of a hot summer, Tiddalik woke with a huge thirst. He drank the water in all the little puddles. But he was still thirsty. He hopped about everywhere and drank all the water in every lake, **bila-bang** (billabong) and **bila** (river).

At last, Tiddalik felt satisfied, so he settled down beneath a large tree to rest his giant body. He knew that with all the water in his belly he would never be thirsty again and he was happy.

But all the other creatures who lived in this vast land were unhappy. Tiddalik had not left them any water, no water at all. The poor animals grew thirstier each day.

Feeling desperate, they went to Tiddalik to talk about their problem.

'Please let a little water spill out for us', they begged.

But Tiddalik said, 'No'.

Bandhaa gathered all the animals together and said, 'We must work as a team to get old greedy Tiddalik to give us some water'. But nobody could think of what to do.

Gugaa the goanna said, 'If we scare Tiddalik he might give us some water', but **wilay** the possum said, 'No, we don't want to be mean'.

Finally, **wambad** the wise old wombat suggested that they try to make the mean old frog laugh. 'If he would only laugh', said **wambad**, 'some of the water he has drunk would come flooding out'.

The animals agreed that this was a good idea and each set about to make the giant frog laugh. They played leapfrog over each other. **Dinawan** the emu did a ballet dance. The dingoes marched two by two to the beat of the tail of old **bandhaa**.

Gugu-ba-rra the kookaburra told stories that were so funny he laughed until he almost choked—but Tiddalik didn't even smile. The wallabies waltzed and the wombats wobbled, but the giant frog ignored every single one of them.

The bush animals were very upset. Then suddenly an eel called **galin-dulin** slithered up to the group. He had left his favourite creek, which was now completely dry, and he was furious!

He went up to Tiddalik and in his eel language began to accuse him. As **galin-dulin** became more and more angry, he twisted his body into strange and incredible shapes. At one stage, he even tied himself into a knot. He looked so comical that Tiddalik began to laugh. It was the first time he had ever laughed.

At first, it was just a chuckle but then a great long loud 'ha ha'. Then, to everyone's delight, the water began to trickle and then to flood from his mouth. It continued to flood out across the land, until the lakes, **bila-bang** and **bila** were all filled to overflowing.

The creatures of the land were overjoyed. The giant frog felt so much better after releasing the water and he decided never ever to do such a selfish thing again.

This story tells our **buraay**, our children, how important it is to save and share water.

plants

Baaliyan
Bulrush

guya
fish

Leaves
were woven into baskets and nets to catch **guya** (fish) and ducks.

baaliyan
bulrush

Shoots
were eaten raw.

Making Baskets

Today, some Wiradjuri women are learning to make baskets, just like the ones people made in the past. They collect **baaliyan** (bulrush) leaves, tear each leaf in two, along its length, and then remove the spongy part of the leaf. They dye the leaves and let them dry. When the women weave the leaves into baskets, they sometimes decorate them with feathers at the same time.

Roots

were dried and ground to make **wigay** (damper).

Ngaa-dhu

Nardoo

Spore capsules
were ground into flour.

walam-wunga
grinding stone

wigay
cake, bread, damper

Nardoo Cakes

Ngaa-dhu is a fern that grows in slow moving or still water. It has spores (tiny seeds) in spore capsules. If they're eaten uncooked, they're poisonous. Wiradjuri people were careful to roast the capsules to remove the poison.

The women used **walam-wunga** (grinding stones) to grind the roasted spore capsules into flour. They then mixed the flour with water to make dough, which they cooked in the ashes of a campfire to make **wigay** (cakes). People also ate the dough raw.

Barrinan

Austral Indigo

narrbang
dillybag

Flowers
were used to make dye to decorate **narrbang** (dillybags) and baskets.

Leaves
were crushed and placed in water. This stunned **guya** (fish), so they were easily caught.

guya
fish

Biyal

River Red Gum

muriin
bark canoe

Small branches

were shaped with **guwingal** (stone axes) and knives into tools or weapons, such as **bargan** (boomerangs).

Small hollow branches were used to make emu callers.

Bark

was cut off the trunk with **guwingal** to make large **muriin** (bark canoes). Men used sticks to help stop the bark from closing as they cut out the canoe.

bargan
boomerang

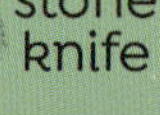

stone knife

Resin

was used as glue when making tools such as knives.

Resin was chewed– it is slightly sweet.

guwingal
stone axe

Barrliyin
Reeds and Rushes

narrbang
dillybag

Leaves
are used to make baskets and **narrbang** (dillybags).
Fresh leaves are plaited or twisted together to make **wayu** (string).

basket

wayu
string

woodlands

Woodlands are the most common habitat in Wiradjuri Country. The main woodland trees are eucalypts and **garal** (our word for wattle trees). Many eucalypts and *garal* have very hard wood, which is good for making weapons and tools. Wiradjuri people used bark for **giigal** (shelters), **gulaman** (dishes), **muriin** (canoes) and **wayu** (string). They used resin for glue and skin lotions. Women collected the seeds of some eucalypts and most wattles to grind into flour to make **wigay** (bread). Other woodland plants provided leaves and stems for string and baskets, and fruit and tubers for food.

In woodlands, scarred trees—where the bark was cut away to make **gulaman** (dishes) and **muriin**—show you where Wiradjuri people have been. The trees didn't die because we removed only some of the bark. Wiradjuri people also cut patterns into the bark on trees. These are called carved trees. Carved trees are now very rare, but you can visit some near Molong, in New South Wales. They are near the grave of Yuranigh, a Wiradjuri man who guided the explorer Major Thomas Mitchell through Wiradjuri Country in the 1840s.

Woodland animals provided Wiradjuri people with meat and skins. **Badhang** (possum skin cloaks) were important for warmth and in cultural events. Many woodland animals rely on trees for food and for homes. Trees have hollows that possums, small bats and many types of birds use for nests. Hollows take more than 100 years to form but, if too many old trees are cut down, some animals may become extinct because there won't be enough hollows for their nests.

Wiradjuri people used to burn **nguram-bang** (Country) to keep it healthy, but only small patches to avoid large fires.

To light the fires, we used **banga-rrung** (firesticks), which were made from wood, such as mulga or cypress pine, that burns easily but lasts for a while. While the small fires were burning, the animals escaped to unburnt country. Fire encourages new plant growth, which provides food for many animals, including kangaroos and wallabies.

Today, we teach scientists and park rangers how to burn **nguram-bang**. Regular burning clears thick understorey so that new seedlings have room to grow. Many of Australia's plants, such as banksias and eucalypts, only release their seeds when fires make them very hot. Burning also helps to get rid of weeds. Small fires help to keep woodlands full of many different native plants and animals.

animals

Wilay

Common Brushtail Possum

Wilay, the common brushtail possum, lives throughout Wiradjuri Country. It eats the leaves of eucalypt trees and also loves the fruit and flowers of other plants.

Wiradjuri men and women made warm **badhang** (cloaks) from **wilay**'s fur. In traditional times, **badhang** kept us warm during **babang** (winter). We burnt beautiful designs onto **badhang**, using a burning stick.

When **bali** (babies) were born, they were wrapped in a possum skin to keep them warm. After each important event, children received another possum skin, which was sewn onto the first one with kangaroo sinew. Eventually, by the time they were adults, they each had a large **badhang**. **Badhang** were decorated with designs and rubbed with ochre and animal fat to protect them.

Today, Wiradjuri women are learning how to make these beautiful, warm **badhang** again.

possum skin in gulaman

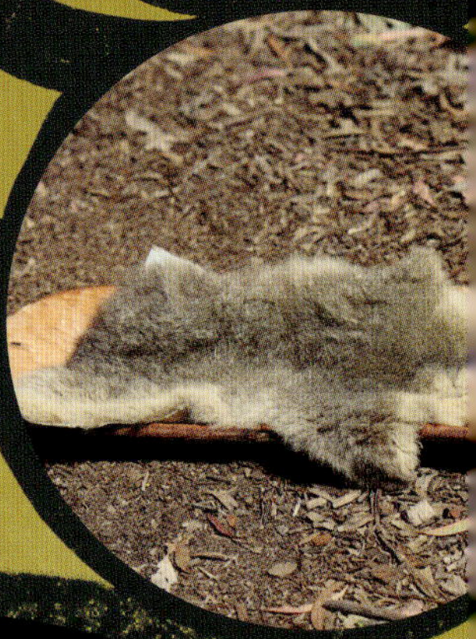

babang
winter

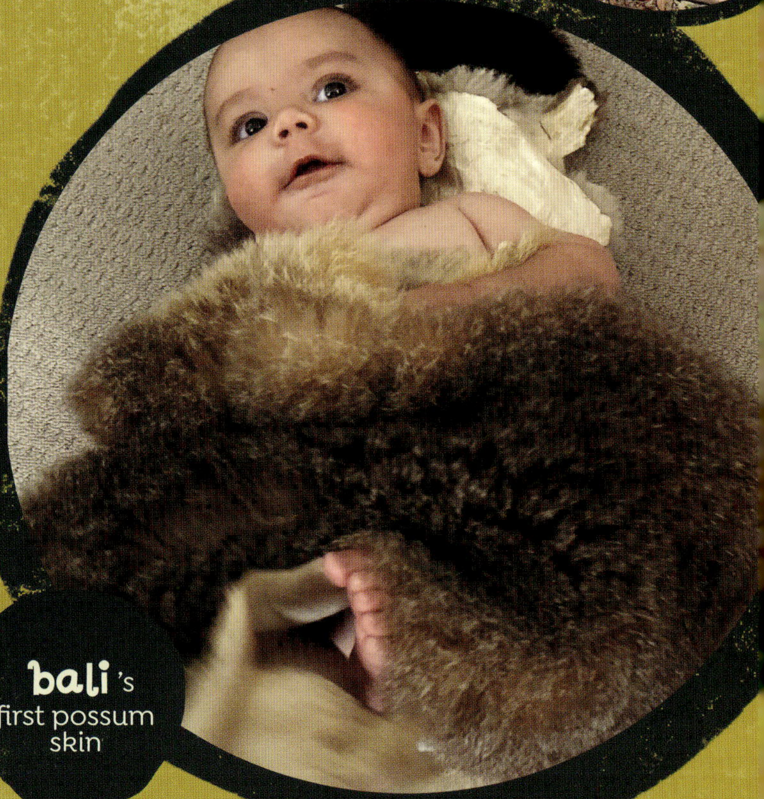

bali's
first possum skin

bali
baby

badhang
possum skin cloak

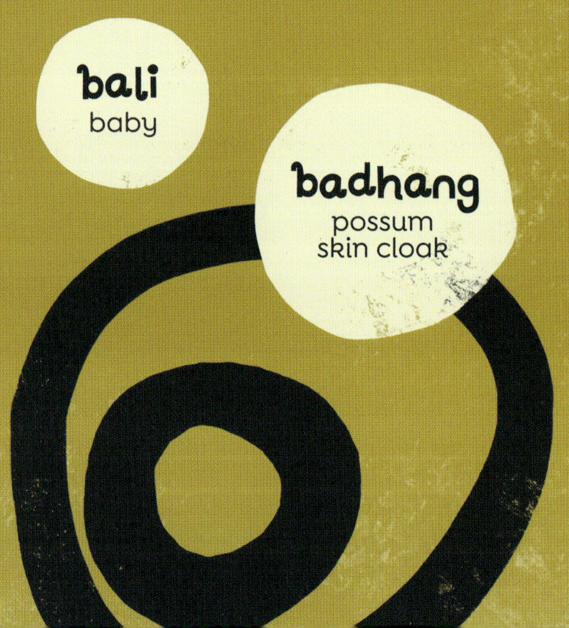

deadly facts Wilay

... is Australia's second largest possum (the cuscus is the largest).

... is nocturnal, so it searches for food—leaves, flowers, fruits and insects—at night. During the day, it sleeps in a tree hollow.

... has a prehensile tail, which means it can use the tail like another hand to grasp branches or to carry nesting material.

... is only 1.5cm long at birth. It climbs into its mother's pouch, where it stays for four or five months. The baby then clings onto its mother's back for a few more months.

... was introduced to New Zealand in the 1830s and is now a pest there. Today, **badhang** are made from New Zealand possums because **wilay** is protected in Australia.

wilay
possum

Gugaa

Goanna (Lace Monitor)

For many Wiradjuri people **gugaa** is a totem animal. The name of our totem plant or animal is passed down through families. Each family or clan is responsible for looking after the totem. Wiradjuri people whose totem is the goanna aren't allowed to eat him. This is a way to make sure that there are always lots of **gugaa** around.

Wiradjuri people who can eat **gugaa** know that the best time to hunt him is when he's been in the trees eating birds' eggs. **Gugaa** is not as tasty if he's been feeding on dead animals.

Gugaa is very oily and we mixed its body fat with ochre to decorate our bodies and to paint on cave walls. Ochre is a type of clay that ranges in colour from yellow to deep orange and brown. The fat made the colours last longer. It was also used as an ointment to relieve aches and pains.

Gugaa features in many of our stories and, in **balanda** (the beginning), he was giant-sized.

gugaa
goanna

balanda
beginning

deadly facts Gugaa

- ... *has powerful claws for climbing trees and for digging.*
- ... *is the only lizard that has a forked tongue, which it uses for sensing prey—insects, other reptiles, small mammals, birds and birds' eggs, and carrion (dead animals).*
- ... *is the second largest lizard in Australia and can grow to over 2m in length.*
- ... *lives alone until it's time to find a mate. The female lays eggs in a termite mound and, around nine months later, the hatchlings dig their way out.*
- ... *stays in tree hollows or under logs or rocks when the weather gets too cool.*

Gugu-ba-rra

Laughing Kookaburra

The word 'kookaburra' comes from the Wiradjuri word **gugu-ba-rra** and is based on the sound of the kookaburra's call. Other Aboriginal Nations have similar words.

Gugu-ba-rra is important to the Wiradjuri because it wakes up the animals early in the morning. We have a story about **gugu-ba-rra** called 'How the sun was made'.

Gugu-ba-rra, like many Australian animals, relies on hollows in eucalypt trees to nest in. If we lose our old eucalypt trees, **gugu-ba-rra** may disappear.

deadly facts Gugu-ba-rra

... is the world's largest kingfisher, but it hardly ever eats fish. It prefers lizards, mammals and frogs.

... perches on a branch and watches the ground below for prey, which it catches with its strong beak.

... lives in families. The younger kookaburras help to defend the family's territory and to look after new chicks.

... laughs to warn other birds to keep out of the family's territory.

wambad
wombat

deadly facts Barran-dha-ng

- ... *lives by itself. It's very quiet, except in the mating season, when the male makes a deep roaring sound to scare off other males.*
- ... *spends around 20 hours a day sleeping and the rest of the time eating eucalyptus leaves. It has special bacteria in its gut to help digest the leaves.*
- ... *drinks water if the weather is really hot, but usually gets enough water from eating leaves and from dew on the leaves.*
- ... *is tiny when it's born and stays in its mother's pouch for about six months. Then it rides on her back for another few months.*
- ... *is related to* **wambad** *(wombat).*

Barran-dha-ng
Koala

The Wiradjuri word for 'koala' is **barran-dha-ng**, but 'koala' comes from the Dharug Nation's word 'gula'. The Dharug Nation is the Aboriginal Nation around western Sydney.

Wiradjuri people respect all animals, including the koala. We didn't hunt **barran-dha-ng** because we believed that a long drought would come if we killed them.

barran-dha-ng
koala

deadly facts Maliyan

- ... *is Australia's largest bird of prey. When spread out, its wings can measure up to 2.5m from one wing tip to the other. The female is larger than the male.*
- ... *can fly high in the sky, riding on currents of warm air.*
- ... *catches live animals with its powerful talons. It also eats carrion—especially animals that have been killed by cars.*
- ... *starts building a new nest with its mate, or fixing up its old nest, around April to May each year. The pair has one to three eggs, but only one chick may survive if there's not a lot of food around.*

Maliyan

Wedge-tailed Eagle

Maliyan, the wedge-tailed eagle, is most common in open woodland, but it's found in other habitats throughout Wiradjuri Country. For some Wiradjuri people, it's a totem animal. It also appears as a constellation in the sky.

Wiradjuri people perhaps followed **maliyan** if they thought she was feeding on prey. If the eagle's catch was fresh, they would take it back to camp to eat.

gambal
bush turkey

gugu-ba-rra
kookaburra

giralang
star

yiraydhuray
morning star (Venus)

yiray
sun

dinawan
emu

balanda
beginning

let me tell you a story

How the sun was made

Back in **balanda** (the beginning), there was no **yiray** (sun). There was only the moon and **giralang** (the stars). **Giralang** were the fires of the sky people. At this time, no people lived on Earth. There were only birds and other animals, which were many sizes larger than they are today.

A long time ago, **dinawan** the emu and **gambal** the bush turkey were on a large plain near the river. As usual, they were arguing. **Dinawan** was jealous that **gambal** could fly, and **gambal** was jealous that **dinawan** had so many babies.

Gambal became very angry and rushed to **dinawan**'s nest. She seized one of the huge eggs and threw it with all her might into the sky. Up, up and up it went until it smashed open on a heap of firewood, which had been gathered by the sky people. The firewood burst into flames as the yellow yolk from **dinawan**'s egg spilled over it.

The flame lit up the world below and the animals on Earth were dazzled by the brightness. The sky people could see all the colours of Earth—the reds, greens, blues and yellows of the birds and flowers—and they could feel the warmth of the fire.

The sky people saw how bright and beautiful Earth looked when lit up by the flames. They thought it would be good to make a fire every night to see the stunning colours. So, all night they collected wood and heaped it into a big pile. When the heap was almost big enough, they would send out **yiraydhuray** (the morning star) to warn those on Earth that the fire would soon be lit.

But the sky people found that **yiraydhuray** did not wake the animals on Earth. So, they decided that there should be a noise at dawn to wake the sleeping animals to tell them that day was coming. Unfortunately, for a long time they couldn't find anyone suitable.

At last, one morning, they heard the sound of something in the distance. At first, it was very faint—'goo goor gaga'—but, as they got closer and closer, it got louder and louder—'goo goor gaga, GOO GOOR GAGA, GOO GOOR GAGA'.

'That's the noise we want,' the sky people said.

As they got even closer, they saw that it was **gugu-ba-rra** the kookaburra.

They asked **gugu-ba-rra** to laugh his loudest every morning before the fire was lit to wake up all the sleepers.

'But what's in it for me?' asked **gugu-ba-rra**.

'Did you like anything about the new fire?' replied the sky people.

'I loved seeing the difference between day and night and I liked seeing the reds, greens, blues and yellows of the birds and the flowers. But most of all I loved warming my wings,' said **gugu-ba-rra**.

'Well, if you agree to laugh every morning, then we will agree to light the fire at the beginning of every day,' said the sky people.

'But won't I get in trouble with the animals here on Earth?' asked **gugu-ba-rra**.

'We'll tell them to treat you like a brother and not to harm you or make fun of you. We'll tell them that your job is important,' said the sky people.

So, **gugu-ba-rra** agreed to laugh his loudest at dawn every day, and he has done this ever since—'goo goor gaga, goo goor gaga, goo goor gaga, gaga ga GOO GOOR GAGA GOO GOOR GAGA GA'.

Wiradjuri people treat **gugu-ba-rra** like a brother because if ever a time comes when he stops laughing before **yiray** rises, darkness will come to Earth again.

plants

Giigandul

Silver Wattle

Seeds

were ground, using **walam-wunga** (grinding stones), into flour for **wigay** (bread).

wigay
cake, damper, bread

walam-wunga
grinding stone

Resin

was mixed with ash to help heal wounds and sores.

It was chewed, then spat out—like chewing gum.

Magga
Mugga Ironbark

Wood
was used for making tools and weapons, such as clap sticks, **ganhay** (digging sticks) and **bargan** (boomerangs).
bargan
boomerang
Baagang
Yellow Box
muriin
canoe
Bark
was cut away to make **muriin** (canoes).
Yellow box bark was better for making **muriin** than the bark of many other eucalypt trees.
ganhay
digging stick
Leaves
were used for making antiseptic liquid to fight against infection.

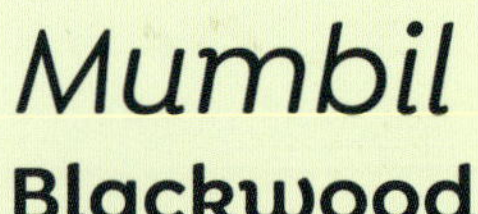

Mumbil
Blackwood

bargan
boomerang

girran girran
shield

guya
fish

Leaves

were crushed up and put in waterholes. The leaves took the oxygen out of the water and stunned **guya** (fish) and other animals so they were easily caught.

wigay
cake, damper, bread

Seeds

were ground into flour for **wigay** (damper).

Bark

was heated in water and then rubbed on aching joints and on cuts and sores.

The bark was also used to make **wayu** (string).

wamar
spear thrower, woomera

Wood

was used for making **bargan** (boomerangs), **wamar** (spear throwers) and **girrangirran** (shields).

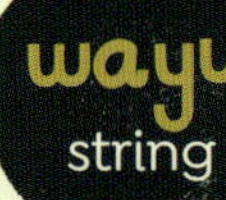

wayu
string

Guwandang
Quandong

Yirany
Yam Daisy

Tubers

were dug up using **ganhay** (digging sticks), cooked over a fire and eaten. They taste a bit like coconut.

ganhay
digging stick

Ngawang

False Sarsaparilla

Leaves

were soaked in warm water to make a sweet drink (the early settlers drank it too and called it bushman's tea).

Stems

were used to weave baskets and to make **wayu** (rope).

guya
fish

wayu
rope

Flowers

on **ngawang** told us it was time to catch the fat **guya** (fish).

Flowers were soaked in water, which was then used to help heal mouth ulcers.

grass lands

In the past, Wiradjuri Country grasslands and plains covered large areas. They were home to many of the plants and animals that we relied on for food, clothing, **giigal** (shelters), medicine, tools and weapons.

Dinawan (emus) provided eggs and meat for food, and feathers for decoration; and kangaroos provided meat, sinews for **wayu** (string) and skins for clothes. The fruit and seeds of grassland plants were part of Wiradjuri people's diet, leaves were used for medicines and fruit was used for dyes.

Now, native grasslands are endangered. Hoofed animals, such as sheep and cattle, and introduced grasses, pasture and weeds, as well as the use of chemicals on crops, have all helped to destroy a lot of Australia's grasslands. Grasslands have also disappeared under new houses and buildings of growing towns and cities.

Wiradjuri people used to burn small areas of grassland, as well as woodland, using **banga-rrung** (firesticks) to light the fires. By burning **nguram-bang** (Country), we helped keep it full of different native plants and animals. The animals were able to flee the flames safely, but returned to the burnt area when the plants had regrown. Fire encourages new plant growth, which attracts many animals, including kangaroos and wallabies.

animals

Dinawan

Emu

Wiradjuri people call the emu **dinawan**. **Dinawan** features in many of our stories, along with **gambal** the bush turkey. **Dinawan** is always jealous of **gambal** because **gambal** can fly, but **dinawan** can't.

Dinawan was good to eat, but to catch an emu we had to make her come close. We used an emu caller to make the sound of an emu. The emu caller was like a small didgeridoo, which we tapped with our hand. We also used a hook boomerang with emu feathers attached to the top so that it looked like a baby emu. Hearing the emu caller and seeing the feathers made the emu think that there was a chick nearby. Because **dinawan** is a very curious bird, she came closer to investigate.

Emu feathers decorated headdresses, dillybags, baskets and belts. Today, some Wiradjuri people use emu feathers for decoration.

Emu eggs were a favourite meal, but we collected only a few from **dinawan**'s nest. We taught our **buraay** (children) not to be greedy and to take only what they needed. We also carved or painted emu eggs.

At night, there is even an emu in the sky. If you look at the dark space in **bila-bang** (the Milky Way), you'll see the shape of **dinawan**. In winter, when we saw the whole emu in the sky, we knew it was time to look for emu eggs.

deadly facts Dinawan

... are Australia's tallest birds and the second tallest birds in the world (the tallest is the ostrich).

... have very small wings and can't fly, but they can run quite fast. Their top speed is about 50km/hr.

... zig zag all over the place to get away from a predator, such as a wedge-tailed eagle.

... females lay eggs on the ground and then leave. The males sit on the eggs and might not drink or eat for weeks, waiting for the eggs to hatch. The young chicks stay with their father for around 18 months.

Wambuwuny
Eastern Grey Kangaroo

Wambuwuny is our name for the eastern grey kangaroo. For some Wiradjuri people **wambuwuny** is their totem, which means that they can't eat him.

Wiradjuri men taught young boys how to track and hunt **wambuwuny**. From about the age of 11, they learned how to use **gama** (spears) and **wamar** (spear throwers). They also learned how to track **wambuwuny** by looking for their footprints. Wiradjuri people knew that the best time to hunt **wambuwuny** was in the middle of the day, when the kangaroos were sleepy. Today, many of us still eat kangaroo as it's a very healthy meat, with very little fat.

Fire was a good way to attract kangaroos. Wiradjuri people burned the grassland so that when the grasses grew again, the kangaroos appeared to eat the new green shoots.

Men used glue and the sinews from **wambuwuny** to attach stones to wooden handles to make **guwingal** (stone axes). We made cloaks from his skin. We often decorated the cloaks using burning sticks.

In their dances, Wiradjuri men and boys copied the movements of kangaroos. This was one way of teaching boys about kangaroo behaviour. Today, some men and boys perform these dances.

The name 'kangaroo' is based on a Guugu Yimithirr word 'gangurru'. The Guugu Yimithirr are Aboriginal people from north Queensland.

kangaroo skin cloak

deadly facts Wambuwuny

... may live in large mobs of up to about 50 kangaroos. From late afternoon to early morning, they graze on grass. During the day, they rest in the shade.

... are good swimmers and may enter water to avoid predators.

... are amazing because, during the breeding season, females may have one baby in the pouch, one hopping alongside them and a tiny embryo inside, beginning to grow.

... can breed quickly when there's lots of food around. In good conditions, as soon as a joey has left the pouch, the embryo is born and makes its way to the mother's pouch.

... are about the size of a jellybean at birth. They stay in the pouch for around nine months, but still drink milk from their mother after they leave the pouch.

gama
spear

wamar
spear thrower

dinawan
emu

gambal
bush turkey, Australian bustard

deadly facts Gambal

... *are Australia's heaviest flying birds. They actually prefer walking.*

... *wander around on their long legs, at night, searching for seeds, buds, fruit, frogs, lizards and invertebrates.*

... *males try to attract females by making roaring noises and by strutting around. Females choose mates that perform the best display.*

... *lay one large olive-green egg and only females look after the chick.*

... *are endangered in New South Wales. Foxes and cats catch them easily because gambal spend most of their time on the ground. And, when there are too many cattle and sheep grazing on the grasslands, their habitat is destroyed.*

Gambal

Bush Turkey (Australian Bustard)

Today, **gambal** (bush turkey) isn't common in Wiradjuri Country, but apparently she was very tasty. She was probably a totem to some Wiradjuri people, because she played an important part in our stories. **Gambal** is always jealous of **dinawan** the emu, because **dinawan** has lots of babies and **gambal** only has a few.

Burralgang

- ... *are tall, long-legged, long-necked birds called cranes. There are only two cranes in Australia—**burralgang** and sarus cranes.*
- ... *have a spectacular dance, in which they jump in the air and spread out their wings. They bob their head and bow and make loud trumpeting sounds.*
- ... *use their strong straight bill to dig in the ground for food, such as roots, large insects and frogs.*
- ... *lay two eggs a year. Both parents look after the eggs and the chicks. The chicks stay in the nest for only a couple of days, but the parents look after them until the next breeding season.*

Burralgang

Brolga

Burralgang the brolga is another character in some of our stories. Like **gambal**, she and dinawan are jealous of each other. **Burralgang** can fly but she doesn't have as many babies as **dinawan**, and **dinawan** has lots of chicks but can't fly.

Wiradjuri people know that **burralgang** loves to dance. Women and girls copied her movements in many of our dances. By copying animals in our dances, we taught our girls about the animals' behaviour. Some women and girls are learning these dances today.

The name 'brolga' comes from the Kamilaroi word 'buralga'. People of the Kamilaroi Nation live north of the Wiradjuri Nation, in northern New South Wales, around the towns of Tamworth and Gunnedah and to just beyond the Queensland border.

let me tell you a story

Dinawan the emu and gambal the bush turkey

gambal
bush turkey

A long time ago in **balanda** (the beginning), **dinawan** the emu and **gambal** the bush turkey were on a large plain near the river. They were always fighting because **gambal** was jealous that **dinawan** could run so well and **dinawan** was jealous that **gambal** could fly so well.

One day **gambal** decided to trick **dinawan**. She folded her wings behind her back and told **dinawan** that she had cut off her wings because she didn't want to be like ordinary birds.

'Any bird can fly,' she said, 'but only special birds walk and run everywhere.'

Dinawan thought about this and decided to cut off his wings as well. He quickly felt his legs get stronger and discovered that he could run much faster.

The next day, he showed **gambal** how special he was. **Gambal** laughed and laughed and then showed **dinawan** that she still had her wings.

'How foolish you are,' said **gambal**. 'It's much better to fly than to run.'

Dinawan was very angry that **gambal** had tricked him.

A long time went by until one day **dinawan** was feeding on the plains with only two of his children. **Gambal** came by with her many **buraay** (children).

'You look very tired,' said **dinawan**. 'That's why I decided to keep only two of my **buraay**. They're much easier to feed and see how large they've grown.'

Gambal saw that **dinawan** was right. The next day she met **dinawan** on the plains.

'Look,' she said. 'I have taken your advice. Now I have only my two largest **buraay**, and they're big and strong.'

Dinawan laughed and called to his other 14 children to show themselves.

'It's much better to have many **buraay** than just a couple,' he said.

This is why today emus have many **buraay** but can't fly, and bush turkeys can fly but only have two **buraay** a year.

plants

Dyurigalgal

Spinifex (Porcupine Grass)

resin

Crystals

at the base of the grass blades, where they join together, were used for making glue, to use in tool- and weapon-making.

Making Glue

At the base of **dyurigalgal** (spinifex) are tiny sticky crystals that look like sugar. Men and women beat **dyurigalgal** to collect the crystals. They then heated the crystals over a fire. The crystals melted into a sticky resin, to which they added bits of grass and ash. It turned into a glue that set rock hard. Men used the glue to attach axe-heads to handles. When they needed the glue to fix tools and weapons, they reheated it to make it soft again.

resin glued the axe-head and handle together

Gaymaan

Kangaroo Grass

Seeds

were ground, using **walam-wunga** (grinding stones), into flour for **wigay** (bread).

wigay
damper

walam-wunga
grinding stone

gulaman
dish

Making Damper

Women collected seeds of **gaymaan** (kangaroo grass) in their **gulaman** (dishes). Back at camp, they ground the seeds using **walam-wunga** (grinding stones) to make flour. They then mixed the flour with water and cooked it in the hot coals of a fire to make **wigay** (damper).

Barrinan
Ruby Saltbush

Fruit

was eaten fresh because it was fleshy and sweet.

It was also used to dye baskets.

Yadhandha

Emu Bush

Biradur

Pigface

Leaves

are fleshy so we chewed them when we were thirsty.

The juice from the leaves was used for burns and blisters.

Flowers and fruit

were eaten raw in late winter and spring.

Bidyuri

Pituri

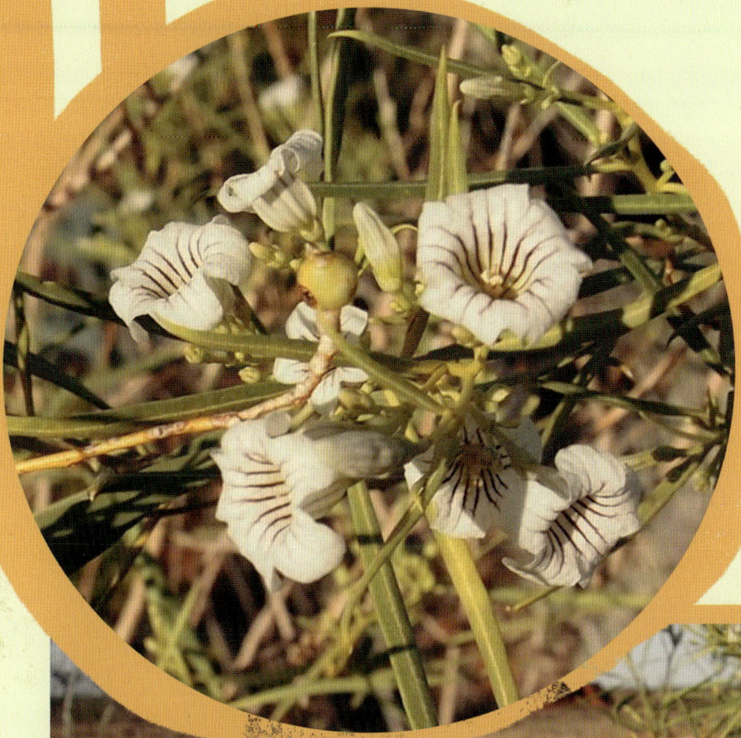

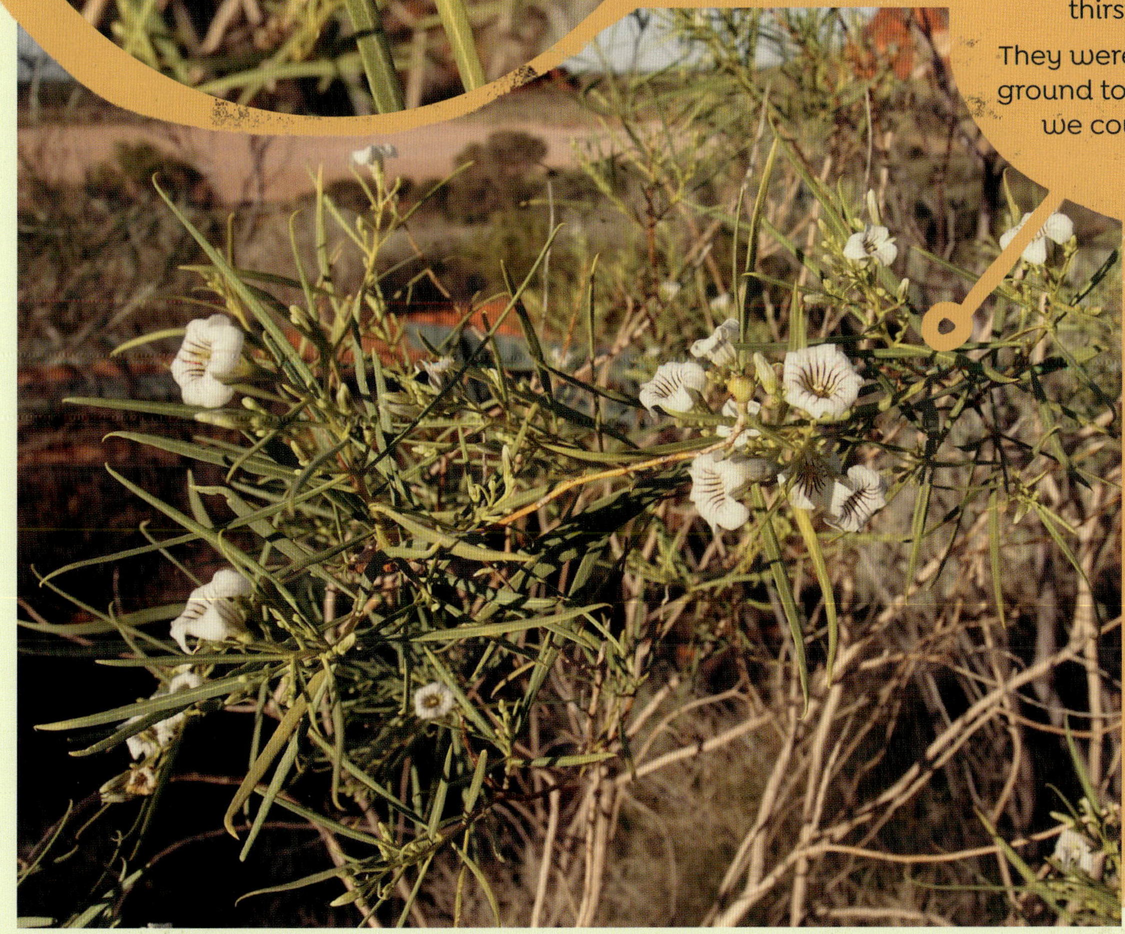

Leaves

were dried and ground together with ash and then chewed to help overcome thirst and hunger.

They were also crushed and ground to stun **guya** (fish) so we could catch them.

guya
fish

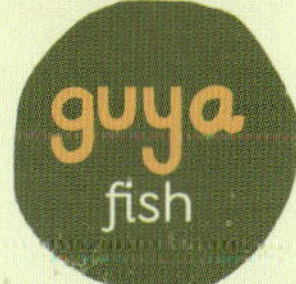

rocky outcrops

In Wiradjuri Country, there are rocky outcrops everywhere, but they're easiest to see in grasslands and woodlands. The name of Molong, a small town in central New South Wales, is based on the Wiradjuri word **malang**, which means rocky area.

yaba
carpet snake

guwingal
stone axe

Many generations of Wiradjuri families used rock overhangs to protect them from the wind, rain and heat. People sometimes created art on the rock in the overhangs in the Great Dividing Range, which you can still see today. The Wollemi National Park, near Mudgee, is one place where you can see rock art.

Handprints on the rock tell us that **buraay** (children) were there. You might also see pictures of tools and weapons, as well as animal tracks, that might be a record of hunting trips. Perhaps the overhang was a place where adults taught **buraay** about animal tracks, stories and rules. Through some of their rock art, Wiradjuri people were showing others that they had been there and that this was their **nguram-bang** (Country). It's hard to know exactly how old the art is, but it's thousands and thousands of years old.

Rocky outcrops also provided rocks for tools such as axes and **walam-wunga** (grinding stones). Men made **guwingal** (stone axes) by chipping off edges of a stone to make it sharper. They then sharpened **guwingal** by scraping each side across rock. Over time, this made grooves in the rock, because the men used the same spot over and over. Axe-grinding grooves are ancient.

When it rained, water collected in natural rock holes. Wiradjuri people used the water and, in some areas, they turned the rock holes into wells by scraping them out with **guwingal** so that they held more water.

In rocky areas, Wiradjuri people hunted various animals for meat or skins, such as **barrbay** (brush-tailed rock wallabies), **walarru** (common wallaroos) and **yaba** (carpet snakes), and they climbed up cliffs to collect eggs laid by peregrine falcons. Every year, the migration of **bugaang** (bogong moths) to the mountains was an important event for the Wiradjuri. This was a time when many Aboriginal Nations came together for ceremonies and to feast on the moths.

Like the plants of river areas, the woodlands and the grasslands, the plants of rocky places gave the Wiradjuri food, as well as wood, bark, leaves and resin to make items they needed.

axe-grinding grooves

handprints rock art

rock water hole

walarru
common wallaroo

bugaang
bogong moth

animals

Walarru

Common Wallaroo

Wiradjuri people call the common wallaroo **walarru.** Wallaroos are larger than wallabies but smaller than kangaroos. They like rock ledges and caves for resting in during the day. Wiradjuri people ate **walarru** and used their skin for clothing.

The name 'wallaroo' probably comes from 'walaru', a word from the Dharug Aboriginal language in the Sydney region. This was the place where European scientists first described the common wallaroo. The Wiradjuri name is very similar.

deadly facts Walarru

- *... is very sturdy and has a longer and shaggier coat than a kangaroo or a wallaby. The male is much bigger than the female and has a very muscular chest.*
- *... hops in a more upright manner than kangaroos.*
- *... grazes on grass, small bushes and other plants during the night.*
- *... spends most of the time on its own.*
- *... gives birth to a tiny joey, who stays with its mother for about nine months.*

walarru
common wallaroo

Barrbay

Brush-tailed Rock Wallaby

Barrbay, brush-tailed rock wallabies, love rocky outcrops. These wallabies live mainly along the Great Dividing Range in the east of Wiradjuri Country. Wiradjuri people hunted **barrbay** for food and they used their skins for making clothing.

deadly facts Barrbay

- *... has a bushier tail than a kangaroo or a wallaby.*
- *... hops from boulder to boulder. It can hop up almost vertical rock faces and can even climb trees.*
- *... uses its long tail to provide balance when hopping on rocks. The rough soles of its feet help it grip onto the rocks.*
- *... lives in a family group.*
- *... rests during the day in a rock shelter and forages at night for grasses, herbs, leaves, flowers, seeds and fruit.*

barrbay
brush-tailed rock wallaby

Yaba

Carpet Snake (Diamond Python)

The carpet snake's name in Wiradjuri is **yaba.** We have many stories about snakes and serpents as we believe they were the creators of our rivers and creeks. In ancient times, snakes were huge animals and were part of Australia's megafauna.

When **yaba** grew to a large size, they became a good source of meat.

deadly facts Yaba

... is found in rock crevices and under logs.

... feeds on small bats that shelter in the crevices and in caves.

... is called a carpet snake because it comes in a variety of different colours and patterns, just like the beautiful carpets woven in Middle Eastern countries.

... isn't venomous. It kills lizards and small mammals by wrapping itself around them and suffocating them. Then yaba swallows its prey whole.

... sleeps during the day and hunts at night.

... lays 10 to 30 eggs and curls around them to keep them warm and to protect them from predators.

Peregrine Falcon

Cliffs and rocky outcrops are good places to see peregrine falcons. They don't build a nest; instead they lay their eggs on cliff edges, which provide protection from predators. Although Wiradjuri people collected their eggs, they never took all of them because they wanted to make sure there were always plenty of peregrine falcons.

We don't know the Wiradjuri word for the peregrine falcon anymore.

deadly facts Peregrine Falcon

... sits on a high perch or circles high over the landscape, watching for prey. It hunts birds, which it catches with its powerful talons in mid-air.

... dives, headfirst, after its prey and can reach speeds of over 320km/hr. This makes it one of the fastest bird species on Earth.

... lays its eggs on a cliff edge or in an abandoned nest of a wedge-tailed eagle or a raven.

Bugaang

Bogong Moth

Bugaang were a very important food source for Wiradjuri people. In spring, millions and millions of the moths fly to the Snowy Mountains. They shelter in rock crevices and caves to protect themselves and to keep cool.

In the past, every year, large numbers of Aboriginal people from neighbouring nations travelled to the mountains to collect, cook and eat the moths. **Bugaang** are very nutritious because they're high in fat and protein. People made fires and cooked the moths quickly on hot ashes to remove the scales and wings. They ate the nutty-tasting moths whole. They also ground some into a paste to make cakes, to keep for later.

deadly facts Bugaang

... migrates large distances each spring —up to 1,000km—at night. It flies to the Australian Alps, in New South Wales and Victoria, from its breeding grounds in large open areas in southern Queensland, western and north-western New South Wales and western Victoria.

... spends the hot summer months in the mountains resting in a kind of hibernation.

... migrates back to its breeding grounds in autumn. It's a mystery how the moths can find their way over such long distances and how they can travel at night.

... is the food of mountain pygmy possums, ravens, bats and other animals. This is a problem because there aren't as many ***bugaang*** *as there used to be. There are several possible reasons why—long droughts, climate change, chemical spraying in the breeding grounds or the distracting lights of cities. These could upset* ***bugaang****'s navigation.*

bugaang
bogong moth

let me tell you a story

The rainbow serpent

balanda
beginning

Milawa
Murray River

Galari
Lachlan River

There are many stories that tell us how the mountains and rocks were formed in **balanda** (the beginning). Often, the stories involve the rainbow serpent who created the mountains and rivers across Wiradjuri Country.

For a long time, the rainbow serpent remained very still underground. This was before **biyaami** (the creator) created all the animals and people on Earth. One day, the serpent awoke and started moving through Wiradjuri Country. He twisted and turned and pushed his way through **nguram-bang** (Country) and, as he did so, he created the winding **bila** (rivers)—**Galari**, **Wambuul**, **Marrambidya** and **Milawa.** He also created the creeks, billabongs and wetlands.

After all this work, the rainbow serpent fell asleep. He is still sleeping and his body forms the Great Dividing Range—the line of mountains to the east of Wiradjuri Country.

plants

Maybal
Grass Tree

dharru-ngarrung
native bee

Flowers

were soaked in water to make a sweet drink.

Young flowers were eaten.

When maybal flowered in late winter and early spring, we knew that **dharru-ngarrung** (native bees) would be in the area.

Flower spikes

were used for **gama** (spears).

The smoke from a burning flower spike was good for colds.

Leaves

were used to make baskets.

Young shoots and leaf bases were eaten.

gama
spear

Resin

was found at the base of leaves and was used for fixing tools and weapons, and for patching **gulaman** (dishes).

Garraa
White Cypress Pine

Wood was used as **banga-rrung** (torches) to carry fire from one place to another. The wood is dense so it burns slowly, which makes it a good torch.

Resin was used as a glue to fix tools and weapons.

Gundhay
Red Stringybark

ganhay
digging stick

Wood
is a reddish colour and was very easy to work with to make tools and weapons, such as **ganhay** (digging sticks) and handles for **guwingal** (stone axe heads).

guwingal
stone axe head

Bark
was stripped off the trunk and woven together to make strong **wayu** (rope).

wayu
string, rope

Garriwang

Spearwood

murri-yang
sky world

sky

For Wiradjuri people, the sky is also part of Country. We call the sky world **murri-yang** and this is where **biyaami** our creator lives. We have many names for the sky and for what we see in the sky. **Yiray** is the sun, **giwang** is the full moon and **bargan-bargan** is the moon when it's shaped like a boomerang. The Milky Way is **bila-bang**.

giwang
full moon

biyaami
creator

nguram-bang
Country

yiraydhuray
morning star (Venus)

We had names for the stars—**giralang**—long before the Greeks and Romans gave their names to the stars and constellations. The stars told us when it was time to collect certain foods or when it was time to travel to search for food. **Yiraydhuray** is our name for the morning star (the planet Venus). The Wiradjuri word for the evening star (also Venus) is **wumba**.

On our long journeys across **nguram-bang** (Country), Wiradjuri people used the stars to help us find our way. Many of today's highways follow these ancient Aboriginal pathways.

We used **giralang** for more than navigation. They reminded us of our laws by showing stories in the sky. Our laws taught us how to behave. Some stories, such as the seven sisters, which we call **dindima,** travelled across Wiradjuri Country and across Australia. The seven sisters are seven stars in the cluster of stars that's known as the Pleiades. Although there are seven stars, we can see only six with the naked eye. Stories, like the story of **dindima**, are very old.

bargan-bargan
(big boomerang) moon when it's the shape of a boomerang

dindima
seven sisters

dinawan
emu on Earth

Gugurmin
Emu

When **dinawan** the emu is in the sky we call him **gugurmin**. His head is near the star constellation of **gibirrgan** (the Southern Cross) in what astronomers call the Coalsack. **Gugurmin**'s long body is the dark space in **bila-bang**, the Milky Way.

When we see **gugurmin**'s body, neck and head in the sky, we know that it's time to collect emu eggs. It's around June and July, in winter, when **dinawan** (the emu on Earth) nests. We only ever take a few eggs so that there are still plenty left to hatch.

When it's harder to see the head and neck of **gugurmin**, we know the eggs are nearly ready to hatch and we don't collect them at that time.

gibirrgan
Southern Cross

bila-bang
Milky Way

Waagan

Crow

Near **gugurmin**, we can see **waagan** the crow. The best time to see **waagan** is in the evening sky in summer. **Waagan** is a star that astronomers know as Canopus, the second brightest star in the night sky. The name 'Canopus' comes from ancient Greek stories.

Our name for **waagan** is based on his call, 'waa, waa'. Stories about the crow remind us to behave well. In the stories, **waagan** is always up to something and can't be trusted.

waagan
crow

waagan
crow

Maliyan
Wedge-tailed Eagle

A red star near **waagan** (the crow) is the eye of **maliyan** the wedge-tailed eagle, Australia's largest bird of prey. You can see **maliyan** in the evening sky in **babang** (winter).

The eye of **maliyan** is in the constellation that the ancient Greeks named Aquila, which is the Latin word for 'eagle'. So, Wiradjuri people weren't the only ones to see an eagle's shape in the sky—the Greeks did too.

Gugaa

Goanna

Gugaa the goanna is in the constellation of Scorpius. **Gugaa**'s tail follows the same line of stars as Scorpius' tail. When this constellation first appears in the evening sky in April, we know that it's not time to eat **gugaa** because, at that time, it's skinny.

But, in spring evenings, when the sky goanna faces down in the west, we know that it's a good time to eat **gugaa** because it has fattened up on birds' eggs and so tastes delicious.

gibirrgan
Southern Cross

gugaa
goanna

giralang
star

mouyi
sulphur-crested cockatoo

Mouyi

Sulphur-crested Cockatoo

Mouyi the cockatoos are the two **giralang** (stars) that point towards **gibirrgan** (the Southern Cross). Scientists call them Alpha and Beta Centauri. The two cockatoos were roosting in a tree when it was lifted into the sky. The cockatoos became **mouyi**, the two pointer stars, and the tree became **gibirrgan**.

let me tell you a story

How the birds got their colours and their songs

In **balanda** (the beginning), a beautiful arch appeared in the sky. It was a **gunhungurraan** (rainbow) and it seemed to take colour from all around. **Gunhungurraan** kept growing and growing until, finally, it exploded and the colours floated in the air. As they slowly drifted towards the ground, the colours changed into all the birds we know today.

Waagan the black crow didn't like the feeling of falling and screamed out, 'waa waaaaah, waa waaaaah'. So waagan stayed black.

Gugu-ba-rra the kookaburra thought the falling feeling was funny and so started to laugh.

Still others thought it was the most beautiful feeling of all, so they spread their wings wide and started to sing the most beautiful songs.

That's how the birds got their colours and their voices, because of that rainbow, way back in **balanda**.

See You Later from Wiradjuri Country

Thank you for coming on a journey with me through Wiradjuri Country. I love sharing my culture and I hope you've enjoyed learning something new.

Anytime you are on **nguram-bang** (Country), look around and you will be amazed at the different plants and animals you see, depending on the season. Aboriginal people have always known that it's important to look after **nguram-bang** because **nguram-bang** looks after us.

You may find marks on trees or grooves in rocks, which were made by Aboriginal people hundreds or even thousands of years ago. Aboriginal people have been on Country for a very long time.

There are nearly 100 Wiradjuri words in this book. Now you know a few words in my language, I hope you are inspired to keep on learning.

guwayu

see you later

Index of Wiradjuri words

(Wiradjuri to English and English to Wiradjuri)

Notes: In the Wiradjuri language, a noun has one form whether it is used in the singular or in the plural. For example, *guwingal* can refer to one stone axe or to many stone axes.

There is no word for 'a' or 'the' in the Wiradjuri language.

Scientific names are provided for the main animals and plants featured in the book.

To learn how to pronounce Wiradjuri words, download the Wiradjuri Language Dictionary phone app, produced by the Wiradjuri Condobolin Corporation Limited. It's free.

WIRADJURI TO ENGLISH

baagang	yellow box *(Eucalyptus melliodora)*
baaliyan	cumbungi *(bulrush)*, all types including narrow-leaf cumbungi *(Typha domingensis)* and broad-leaf cumbungi *(Typha orientalis)*
babang	winter
badhang	possum-skin cloak
balanda	beginning
bali	baby
bandhaa	red kangaroo
banga-rrung	firestick, torch
bargan	boomerang
bargan-bargan	crescent-shaped boomerang, crescent-shaped moon
barran-dha-ng	koala *(Phascolarctos cinereus)*
barrbay	brush-tailed rock wallaby *(Petrogale penicillata)*
barrinan	small bush—in this book, barrinan means either Austral indigo *(Indigofera australis)* or ruby saltbush *(Enchylaena tomentosa)*
barrliyin	reeds and rushes
bidyuri	pituri *(Duboisia hopwoodii)*
bila	river
bila-bang	billabong, the Milky Way
bila-durang	platypus *(Ornithorhynchus anatinus)*
biradur	pigface *(Sarcozona praecox)*
biyaami	creator
biyal	river red gum *(Eucalyptus camaldulensis)*
budhanbang	Pacific black duck *(Anas superciliosa)*
bugaang	bogong moth *(Agrotis infusa)*
bugang	necklace
buraay	child
burralgang	brolga *(Grus rubicunda)*
dharru-ngarrung	native bee

dinawan	emu *(Dromaius novaehollandiae)*
dindima	seven sisters
dyirri-dyirr	willy wagtail
dyurigalgal	spinifex, porcupine grass *(Triodia scariosa)*
gagalin	yellow belly, golden perch *(Macquaria ambigua)*
Galari	Lachlan River
galin-dulin	eel (any species)
gama	spear
gambal	bush turkey, Australian bustard *(Ardeotis australis)*
gandhalwurr	broad-shelled turtle
ganhay	digging stick (a woman's)
garal	wattle tree
garraa	white cypress pine *(Callitris glaucophylla)*
garriwang	spearwood *(Acacia doratoxylon)*
gaymaan	kangaroo grass *(Themeda triandra)*
gibirrgan	Southern Cross
giigal	shelter
giigandul	silver wattle *(Acacia dealbata)*
giralang	star
girrangirran	shield
giwang	full moon
gudhamang	eastern long-necked turtle *(Chelodina longicollis)*
gudhamang-dhuray	having turtles
gugaa	goanna, lace monitor *(Varanus varius)*
gugu-ba-rra	laughing kookaburra *(Dacelo novaeguineae)*
gugurmin	emu (in the sky)
gulaman	coolamon, bark or wood dish
gundhay	red stringybark *(Eucalyptus macrorhyncha)*
gunhungurraan	rainbow

guwandang	quandong *(Santalum acuminatum)*
guwayu	see you later
guwingal	stone axe
guya	fish (any species)
magga	mugga ironbark *(Eucalyptus sideroxylon)*
malang	rocky area
maliyan	wedge-tailed eagle *(Aquila audax)*
Marrambidya	Murrumbidgee River
maybal	grass tree *(Xanthorrhoea glauca)*
Milawa (at Albury, Yindi above Albury)	Murray River
mouyi	sulphur-crested cockatoo (the two pointer stars, Alpha and Beta Centauri, of the Southern Cross)
mumbil	blackwood *(Acacia melanoxylon)*
munun	water rat
muriin	bark canoe
murri-yang	sky world
nalanala	club (a weapon of war, with a thick knob on the end)
narrbang	dillybag
ngaa-dhu	nardoo *(Marsilea drummondii)*
ngawang	false sarsaparilla *(Hardenbergia violacea)*
ngugug	boobook owl
nguram-bang	Country
waagan	crow, Australian raven
waawii	bunyip
walam-wunga	grinding stone
walarru	common wallaroo *(Macropus robustus)*
wamar	spear thrower
wambad	wombat
Wambuul	Macquarie River

wambuwuny	eastern grey kangaroo *(Macropus giganteus)*
warramba	Murray turtle
wayu	string, rope
wigay	bread, cake, damper
wilay	common brushtail possum *(Trichosurus vulpecula)*
wumba	evening star (Venus)
yaanharra	three-pronged spear
yaba	carpet snake, diamond python *(Morelia spilota)*
yabi	yabby, common *(Cherax destructor)*
yadhandha	emu bush *(Eremophila longifolia)*
yirany	yam daisy (*Microseris lanceolata* or any other *Microseris* species)
yiray	sun
yiraydhuray	morning star (Venus)

Austral indigo *(Indigofera australis)*	barrinan
axe (made of stone)	guwingal
baby	bali
bag, dillybag	narrbang
bee (native bee)	dharru-ngarrung
beginning	balanda
billabong, the Milky Way	bila-bang
black duck (Pacific black duck, *Anas superciliosa*)	budhanbang
blackwood *(Acacia melanoxylon)*	mumbil
bogong moth *(Agrotis infusa)*	bugaang
boobook owl	ngugug
boomerang	bargan
bread, cake, damper	wigay
broad-shelled turtle	gandhalwurr
brolga *(Grus rubicunda)*	burralgang
brush-tailed rock wallaby *(Petrogale penicillata)*	barrbay
brushtail possum (common brushtail possum, *Trichosurus vulpecula*)	wilay
bulrush (cumbungi), all types including narrow-leaf cumbungi (*Typha domingensis*) and broad-leaf cumbungi (*Typha orientalis*)	baaliyan
bunyip	waawii
bush turkey, Australian bustard *(Ardeotis australis)*	gambal
cake, bread, damper	wigay
canoe, bark	muriin
carpet snake, diamond python *(Morelia spilota)*	yaba

child, children	buraay
cloak (possum-skin cloak)	badhang
club (a weapon of war, with a thick knob on the end)	nalanala
coolamon, bark or wood dish	gulaman
Country	nguram-bang
creator	biyaami
crow, Australian raven	waagan
cumbungi (bulrush), all types including narrow-leaf cumbungi (*Typha domingensis*) and broad-leaf cumbungi (*Typha orientalis*)	baaliyan
cypress pine (white cypress pine, *Callitris glaucophylla*)	garraa
damper, bread, cake	wigay
digging stick (a woman's)	ganhay
dillybag	narrbang
dish (bark or wood), coolamon	gulaman
duck (Pacific black duck, *Anas superciliosa*)	budhanbang
eagle (wedge-tailed eagle, *Aquila audax*)	maliyan
eastern long-necked turtle *(Chelodina longicollis)*	gudhamang
eel (any species)	galin-dulin
emu (on Earth) *(Dromaius novaehollandiae)*	dinawan
emu (in the sky)	gugurmin
emu bush *(Eremophila longifolia)*	yadhandha
falcon (peregrine falcon, *Falco peregrinus*)	–
false sarsaparilla *(Hardenbergia violacea)*	ngawang
firestick	banga-rrung
fish (any species)	guya

goanna, lace monitor *(Varanus varius)*	gugaa
grass, kangaroo *(Themeda triandra)*	gaymaan
grass tree (*Xanthorrhoea glauca*)	maybal
grey kangaroo (eastern grey kangaroo, *Macropus giganteus*)	wambuwuny
grinding stone	walam-wunga
gum (river red gum, *Eucalyptus camaldulensis*)	biyal
indigo (Austral indigo, *Indigofera australis*)	barrinan
ironbark (mugga ironbark, *Eucalyptus sideroxylon*)	magga
kangaroo grass *(Themeda triandra)*	gaymaan
kangaroo (eastern grey kangaroo, *Macropus giganteus*)	wambuwuny
kangaroo (red kangaroo)	bandhaa
koala *(Phascolarctos cinereus)*	barran-dha-ng
kookaburra (laughing kookaburra, *Dacelo novaeguineae*)	gugu-ba-rra
Lachlan River	Galari
laughing kookaburra (*Dacelo novaeguineae*)	gugu-ba-rra
Macquarie River	Wambuul
Milky Way, billabong	bila-bang
moon (crescent-shaped moon)	bargan-bargan
moon (full moon)	giwang
moth (bogong moth, *Agrotis infusa*)	bugaang
mugga ironbark *(Eucalyptus sideroxylon)*	magga
Murray River	Milawa (at Albury, Yindi above Albury)
Murray turtle	warramba
Murrumbidgee River	Marrambidya
nardoo *(Marsilea drummondii)*	ngaa-dhu
necklace	bugang

owl (boobook owl)	ngugug
pigface *(Sarcozona praecox)*	biradur
pituri *(Duboisia hopwoodii)*	bidyuri
platypus *(Ornithorhynchus anatinus)*	bila-durang
porcupine grass, spinifex *(Triodia scariosa)*	dyurigalgal
possum-skin cloak	badhang
possum (common brush-tail possum, *Trichosurus vulpecula*)	wilay
quandong *(Santalum acuminatum)*	guwandang
rainbow	gunhungurraan
rat (water rat)	munun
red kangaroo	bandhaa
red stringybark *(Eucalyptus macrorhyncha)*	gundhay
reeds and rushes	barrliyin
river	bila
river red gum *(Eucalyptus camaldulensis)*	biyal
rock wallaby (brush-tailed rock wallaby, *Petrogale penicillata*)	barrbay
rocky area	malang
ruby saltbush *(Enchylaena tomentosa)*	barrinan
sarsaparilla (false sarsaparilla, *Hardenbergia violacea*)	ngawang
see you later	guwayu
seven sisters	dindima
shelter	giigal
shield	girrangirran
shrub (small shrub—in this book, barrinan means either Austral indigo, *Indigofera australis*, or ruby saltbush, *Enchylaena tomentosa*)	barrinan

silver wattle *(Acacia dealbata)*	giigandul
sky world	murri-yang
snake (carpet snake, diamond python, *Morelia spilota*)	yaba
Southern Cross	gibirrgan
spear	gama
spear thrower	wamar
spear (three-pronged spear)	yaanharra
spearwood *(Acacia doratoxylon)*	garriwang
spinifex, porcupine grass *(Triodia scariosa)*	dyurigalgal
star	giralang
star (evening star, Venus)	wumba
star (morning star, Venus)	yiraydhuray
stone axe	guwingal
stone (grinding stone)	walam-wunga
string, rope	wayu
stringybark (red stringybark, *Eucalyptus macrorhyncha*)	gundhay
sulphur-crested cockatoo (the two pointer stars, Alpha and Beta Centauri, of the Southern Cross)	mouyi
sun	yiray
turkey (bush turkey, Australian bustard, *Ardeotis australis*)	gambal
turtle (broad-shelled turtle)	gandhalwurr
turtle (eastern long-necked turtle, *Chelodina longicollis*)	gudhamang
turtle (Murray turtle)	warramba
turtles (having turtles)	gudhamang-dhuray
wallaroo (common wallaroo, *Macropus robustus*)	walarru

water rat	munun
wattle tree	garal
wattle (silver wattle, *Acacia dealbata*)	giigandul
wedge-tailed eagle	maliyan
white cypress pine *(Callitris glaucophylla)*	garraa
willy wagtail	dyirri-dyirri
winter	babang
wombat	wambad
yabby (common yabby, *Cherax destructor*)	yabi
yam daisy *(Microseris lanceolata* and other *Microseris* species)	yirany
yellow belly, golden perch *(Macquaria ambigua)*	gagalin
yellow box *(Eucalyptus melliodora)*	baagang

References

Banks, Kirsten, 'Aboriginal Astronomy Can Teach Us about the Link between Sky and Land', *The Guardian,* 21 May 2018. Viewed 3 August 2020 at theguardian.com/commentisfree/2018/may/21/aboriginal-astronomy-can-teach-us-about-the-link-between-sky-and-land

Big Skies Collaboration: Wiradjuri Constellation Art, 14 February 2019. Viewed 3 August 2020 at bigskiescollaboration.wordpress.com/projects/wiradjuri-constellation-art/

Fraser, Ian and Gray, Jeannie, *Australian Bird Names: A Complete Guide.* Collingwood, Vic.: CSIRO Publishing, 2013.

Fuller, Robert S., 'How Ancient Aboriginal Star Maps Have Shaped Australia's Highway Network', *The Conversation,* 7 April 2016. Viewed 3 August 2020 at theconversation.com/how-ancient-aboriginal-star-maps-have-shaped-australias-highway-network-55952

Grant, Stan and Rudder, John, *A New Wiradjuri Dictionary.* O'Connor, ACT: Restoration House, 2010. (Also available as a phone application, *Wiradjuri Language Dictionary.*)

Grant, Stan (Snr) and Rudder, John, *Wiradjuri Language: How It Works: A Grammar in Everyday English.* O'Connor, ACT: Restoration House, 2001.

McKay, Helen F. (ed.), *Gadi Mirrabooka: Australian Aboriginal Tales from the Dreaming,* retold by Pauline E. McLeod, Francis Firebrace Jones and June E. Barker. Englewood, Colorado: Libraries Unlimited, 2001.

Michael, Damian and Lindenmayer, David B., *Rocky Outcrops in Australia.* Clayton South, Vic.: CSIRO Publishing, 2018.

Williams, Alice and Sides, Tim, *Wiradjuri Plant Use in the Murrumbidgee Catchment.* Wagga Wagga, NSW: Murrumbidgee Catchment Management Authority, 2008.

List of Illustrations

Illustrations on the following pages are courtesy of Kristie Peters: front cover, back cover, 12, 28, 46, and 62.

Illustrations on the following pages are courtesy of Scott Sauce Towney: endpapers, 70, 71, 72, 73, 74.

Photographs on the following pages are courtesy of Denise Fowler:

iv (both), 4–5 (background and insets), 6 (top), 8 (top), 11 (top), 15 (top), 16 (bottom), 17 (top left), 17 (bottom), 18 (bottom left), 18 (top right), 19 (bottom), 20–21 (background and insets), 22, 25, 30, 31 (top right), 31 (bottom left), 32 (bottom right), 33 (top), 34 (main image), 34 (bottom left), 34 (bottom right), 37 (top), 40, 41 (second from top), 41 (bottom), 42 (top), 43 (artwork on kangaroo cloak courtesy of Lynette Riley), 48 (top and bottom), 49 (bottom), 54–55 (background and insets), 64 (top right), 65, 66 (top), 67 (right), 77.

Photographs from other sources:

Rivers

6 (bottom) JohnCarnemolla, *Tasmania, Platypus Eating Worm*, 2017, iStock image 658344154; **7** slowmotiongli, *Platypus, Ornithorhynchus anatinus, Den Entrance, Australia*, 2020, iStock image 1250419818; **8** (bottom) Department of Agriculture and Fisheries Queensland, *Golden Perch*, www.nativefish.asn.au/home/page/Golden-Perch; **9** John Cooper, *Eastern Long-necked Turtle, Cowra, New South Wales*, 1995, National Library of Australia Pictures Collection; **10** Catching the Eye, *Cherax destructor, Common Yabbie, Gravid, Australia*, 2012, www.flickr.com/photos/160417453@N04/27079552238/, reproduced under CC BY 2.0: creativecommons.org/licenses/by/2.0/; **11** (left) Ed Dunens, *Pacific Black Duck*, 2016, www.flickr.com/photos/blackswan/30527966044/, reproduced under CC BY 2.0: creativecommons.org/licenses/by/2.0/; **14** Harry Rose, *Typha domingensis–Narrow-leaved Cumbungi*, 2017, www.flickr.com/photos/macleaygrassman/33600843544/, reproduced under CC BY 2.0: creativecommons.org/licenses/by/2.0/; **15** (bottom) Barb Dobson, *Typha domingensis Root*, anthropologyfromtheshed.com/project/edible-roots-typha-bulrush/, courtesy Dr Barb Dobson and Ken Macintyre; **16** (top) Murray Fagg, *Marsilea drummondii, Showing Sporocarps*, 1979, Australian Plant Image Index, © M. Fagg, 1979; **17** (top right) Steve Bittinger, *Indigofera australis, Native Indigo*, 2011, www.flickr.com/photos/sbittinger/6184639317/, reproduced under CC BY 2.0: creativecommons.org/licenses/by/2.0/; **18** (top) Margaret Donald, *River Red Gums, Eucalyptus camaldulensis, the Murrumbidgee River in Flood*, 2016, commons.wikimedia.org/wiki/File:Eucalyptus_camaldulensis_DSC_5750_(29086898504).jpg, reproduced under CC BY 2.0: creativecommons.org/licenses/by/2.0/; **18** (bottom) Cowirrie, *Eucalypt Resin*, 2014, www.flickr.com/photos/111339831@N02/17131789141/, reproduced under CC BY-SA 2.0: creativecommons.org/licenses/by-sa/2.0/; **19** (top) John Tann, *Phragmites in Water*, 2009, www.flickr.com/photos/31031835@N08/3358870819, reproduced under CC BY 2.0: creativecommons.org/licenses/by/2.0/.

Woodlands

23 Doug Beckers, *Brushtail Possum*, 2012, www.flickr.com/photos/dougbeckers/6822269507/, reproduced under CC BY-SA 2.0: creativecommons.org/licenses/by-sa/2.0/; **24** John Tann, *Goanna, or Lace Monitor, Varanus varius*, 2014, www.flickr.com/photos/31031835@N08/12007991124, reproduced under CC BY 2.0: creativecommons.org/licenses/by/2.0/; **26** Fairy Duff, *Koala*, 2010, www.flickr.com/photos/145874413@N08/32259440831; **27** (left) Laurie Boyle, *Wedge-tailed Eagle*, 2013, www.flickr.com/photos/92384235@N02/9476631069/, reproduced under CC BY-SA 2.0: creativecommons.org/licenses/by-sa/2.0/; **27** (right) Laurie Boyle, *Wedge-tailed Eagle*, 2014, www.flickr.com/photos/92384235@N02/14309884992/, reproduced under CC BY-SA 2.0: creativecommons.org/licenses/by-sa/2.0/; **31** (top left) John Tann, *Silver Wattle Flower*, 2011, www.flickr.com/photos/31031835@N08/6280768389, reproduced under CC BY 2.0: creativecommons.org/licenses/by/2.0/; **31** (bottom right) Patrick_K59, *Acacia dealbata*, 2015, commons.wikimedia.org/wiki/File:Silver_Wattle_resin_(16407198081).jpg, reproduced under CC BY 2.0: creativecommons.org/licenses/by/2.0/; **32** (left) John Robert McPherson, *Eucalyptus sideroxylon*, 2015, commons.wikimedia.org/wiki/File:Eucalyptus_sideroxylon_bark_7th_Brigade_Park_Chermside_L1030098.jpg, reproduced under CC BY-SA 4.0: creativecommons.org/licenses/by-sa/4.0/deed.en; **32** (top) Forest and Kim Starr, *Eucalyptus sideroxylon (Red Ironbark)*, 2009, www.flickr.com/photos/starr-environmental/24666936150, reproduced under CC BY 2.0: creativecommons.org/licenses/by/2.0/; **33** (bottom left) Harry Rose, *Eucalyptus melliodora Trunk*, 2019, www.flickr.com/photos/macleaygrassman/48670546316, reproduced under CC BY 2.0: creativecommons.org/licenses/by/2.0/; **33** (bottom right) Max Li, *Eucalyptus melliodora*, 2017, www.flickr.com/photos/140790241@N02/37639274136/; **34** (top) Eric in SF, *Acacia melanoxylon*, 2010, commons.wikimedia.org/wiki/File:Acacia_melanoxylon.jpg, reproduced under CC BY-SA 3.0: creativecommons.org/licenses/by-sa/3.0/deed.en; **34** (middle right) Eric in SF, *Seeds of Acacia melanoxylon*, 2007, commons.wikimedia.org/wiki/File:Acacia_melanoxylon_Seeds.jpg, reproduced under CC BY-SA 3.0: creativecommons.org/licenses/by-sa/3.0/deed.en; **35** (top) denispin, *Quandong Tree in Fruit*, 2015, www.flickr.com/photos/82134796@N03/22306012563/, reproduced under CC BY-ND 2.0: creativecommons.org/licenses/by-nd/2.0/; **35** (bottom) JennyKS, *Quandong (Santalum acuminatum) Fruit and Seeds*, 2011, commons.wikimedia.org/wiki/

File:Quandong_(Santalum_acuminatum)_fruit_%26_seeds.JPG, reproduced under CC BY-SA 3.0: creativecommons.org/licenses/by-sa/3.0/deed.en; **36** (left) Lorraine Oliver, *Microseris lanceolata*, 2010, www.flickr.com/photos/nswgrassyecosystems/5141462965/, reproduced under CC BY-SA 2.0: creativecommons.org/licenses/by-sa/2.0/; **36** (right) A.N. Schmidt-Lebuhn, *Microseris lanceolata*, 2012, © Centre for Australian National Biodiversity Research, 2012; **37** (bottom) John Tann, *Hardenbergia violacea*, 2013, www.flickr.com/photos/31031835@N08/9413929921/, reproduced under CC BY 2.0: creativecommons.org/licenses/by/2.0/.

Grasslands

38–39 John Tann, *Kangaroo Grass*, 2009, www.flickr.com/photos/31031835@N08/3211364780, reproduced under CC BY 2.0: creativecommons.org/licenses/by/2.0/; **41** (top) John Tann, *Emu Footprints*, 2009, www.flickr.com/photos/31031835@N08/3214562823, reproduced under CC BY 2.0: creativecommons.org/licenses/by/2.0/; **41** (middle left) Cathy Stanley-Erickson, *Daddy Emu Sitting on Eggs*, 2010, www.flickr.com/photos/madcitycat/4283983448/, reproduced under CC BY-ND 2.0: creativecommons.org/licenses/by-nd/2.0/; **42** (bottom) John Tann, *Kangaroo Prints*, 2009, www.flickr.com/photos/31031835@N08/3215419240, reproduced under CC BY 2.0: creativecommons.org/licenses/by/2.0/; **44** Graham Winterflood, *Australian Bustard (Ardeotis australis)*, 2017, www.flickr.com/photos/126953422@N04/37037480793, reproduced under CC BY-SA 2.0: creativecommons.org/licenses/by-sa/2.0/; **45** Graham Winterflood, *Brolga (Grus rubicunda)*, 2017, www.flickr.com/photos/126953422@N04/36320751162/, reproduced under CC BY-SA 2.0: creativecommons.org/licenses/by-sa/2.0/; **48** (middle) Harry Rose, *Triodia scariosa*, 2012, www.flickr.com/photos/macleaygrassman/9514666186, reproduced under CC BY 2.0: creativecommons.org/licenses/by/2.0/; **49** (top) John Tann, *Kangaroo Grass*, 2009, www.flickr.com/photos/31031835@N08/3211364780, reproduced under CC BY 2.0: creativecommons.org/licenses/by/2.0/; **49** (middle) John Tann, *Kangaroo Grass Field*, 2009, www.flickr.com/photos/ 31031835@N08/3215313816/, reproduced under CC BY 2.0: creativecommons.org/licenses/by/2.0/; **50** (top) Julie Burgher, *Enchylaena tomentosa var. tomentosa*, 2012, www.flickr.com/photos/sunphlo/7169314710, reproduced under CC BY-ND 2.0: creativecommons.org/licenses/by-nd/2.0/; **50** (bottom) Margaret Donald, *Enchylaena tomentosa, Couradda Road, Edgeroi*, 2019, www.flickr.com/photos/13639096@N06/48083040472, reproduced under CC BY-SA 2.0: creativecommons.org/licenses/by-sa/2.0/; **51** (left) John Tann, *Emu Bush, Eremophila longifolia*, 2014, www.flickr.com/photos/31031835@N08/15301764483, reproduced under CC BY 2.0: creativecommons.org/licenses/by/2.0/; **51** (right) Michael Somerville, *Eremophila longifolia*, 2013, www.flickr.com/photos/80286256@N03/9874176584, reproduced under CC BY-ND 2.0: creativecommons.org/licenses/by-nd/2.0/; **52** (top) Attila Kapitany, *Pigface Bush*, courtesy Attila Kapitany; **52** (bottom) Attila Kapitany, *Pigface Fruit*, courtesy Attila Kapitany; **53** Mark Marathon, *Duboisia hopwoodii*, 2014, commons.wikimedia.org/wiki/File:Duboisia_hopwoodii.jpg, reproduced under CC BY-SA 3.0: creativecommons.org/licenses/by-sa/3.0/deed.en.

Rocky Outcrops

56 stephenallen75, *Dry Land Wallaroo*, 2014, iStock image 529402069; **57** (top) Ken Griffiths, *Pair of Common Wallaroos Drinking*, 2020, iStock image 1227054583; **57** (bottom) Michael Barritt and Karen May, *Macropus robustus*, 2007, commons.wikimedia.org/wiki/File:Macropus_robustus2.jpg, reproduced under CC BY-SA 2.0: creativecommons.org/licenses/by-sa/2.0/deed.en; **58** Doug Beckers, *Brush-tailed Rock Wallaby*, 2011, www.flickr.com/photos/dougbeckers/5849889238, reproduced under CC BY-SA 2.0: creativecommons.org/licenses/by-sa/2.0/; **59** Doug Beckers, *Diamond Python*, 2008, www.flickr.com/photos/dougbeckers/5662151435, reproduced under CC BY-SA 2.0: creativecommons.org/licenses/by-sa/2.0/; **60** Ed Dunens, *Peregrine Falcon*, 2016, www.flickr.com/photos/blachswan/25336773440, reproduced under CC-BY 2.0: creativecommons.org/licenses/by/2.0/; **61** Donald Hobern, *Agrotis infusa*, 2017, www.flickr.com/photos/dhobern/23906548718, reproduced under CC-BY 2.0: creativecommons.org/licenses/by/2.0/; **64** (top left) RuthP, *Xanthorrhoea glauca*, 2020, www.flickr.com/photos/stitchingbushwalker/50266137323, reproduced under CC BY-SA 2.0: creativecommons.org/licenses/by-sa/2.0/; **64** (bottom) John Tann, *Xanthorrhoea glauca after Fire*, 2014, www.flickr.com/photos/31031835@N08/11879064853/, reproduced under CC-BY 2.0: creativecommons.org/licenses/by/2.0/; **66** (bottom) Danielle Langlois, *Red Stringybark (Eucalyptus macrorhyncha)*, 2005, commons.wikimedia.org/wiki/File:Eucalyptus_macrorhyncha_01.jpg, reproduced under CC BY-SA 3.0: creativecommons.org/licenses/by-sa/3.0/deed.en; **66** (right) *Bidgee, Red Stringybark (Eucalyptus macrorhyncha) Bark*, 2009, commons.wikimedia.org/wiki/File:Eucalyptus_macrorhyncha_bark.jpg, reproduced under CC BY-SA 3.0: creativecommons.org/licenses/by-sa/3.0/deed.en; **67** (top) Neil Blair, *Seed Pods of Acacia doratoxylon*, 2021, courtesy Royal Botanic Gardens Victoria; **67** (main) Murray Fagg, *Acacia doratoxylon*, 1990, Australian Plant Image Index a.9957, © M. Fagg, 1990.

Sky

68–73 (background) Eddie Yip, *The Southern Cross*, 2016, www.flickr.com/photos/eddiextcteam/28022078720, reproduced under CC BY-SA 2.0: creativecommons.org/licenses/by-sa/2.0/.

Author's Note: Mandaang guwu—Thank you

I would like to thank the following individuals for their contribution to the creation of this book—Uncle Stan Grant and John Rudder for the Wiradjuri dictionary, Helen Worsley, Adam Shipp, and all of my Wiradjuri Elders, brothers and sisters who I have learnt from over the years. I would also like to thank Publisher Susan Hall for supporting this book, Kristie Peters and Scott Sauce Towney for their wonderful illustrations and my partner Denise Fowler, who encouraged me with this project.

Publisher's Note

Wiradjuri Country is vast. The people of the three rivers are the largest Aboriginal group in New South Wales. The National Library of Australia acknowledges that there are many different ways of relating to Country and living on Country. This is Uncle Larry Brandy's.

Editor's Note

The spelling of Wiradjuri language words in this book follows Stan Grant and John Rudder's *A New Wiradjuri Dictionary*, published by Restoration House in 2010.

Published by NLA Publishing
Canberra ACT 2600

ISBN: 9781922507525

The National Library of Australia acknowledges Australia's First Nations Peoples—the First Australians—as the Traditional Owners and Custodians of this land and gives respect to the Elders—past and present—and through them to all Australian Aboriginal and Torres Strait Islander people.

Editor: Joanna Karmel
Designer: Keisha Leon
Printed in China by Asia Pacific Offset

Find out more about NLA Publishing at nla.gov.au/national-library-publishing.

A catalogue record for this book is available from the National Library of Australia.